# MEGA Early Childhood Education (064) Exam

"You never fail until you stop trying" - Albert Einstein

For inquiries;
info@xmprep.com

# MEGA Early Childhood Education (064) Exam #1

## Test Taking Tips

☐ Take a deep breath and relax

☐ Read directions carefully

☐ Read the questions thoroughly

☐ Make sure you understand what is being asked

☐ Go over all of the choices before you answer

☐ Paraphrase the question

☐ Eliminate the options you know are wrong

☐ Check your work

☐ Think positively and do your best

## Table of Contents

# TEST DIRECTION

DIRECTIONS

Read the questions carefully and then choose the ONE best answer to each question.

Be sure to allocate your time carefully so you are able to complete the entire test within the testing session. You may go back and review your answers at any time.

You may use any available space in your test booklet for scratch work.

Questions in this booklet are not actual test questions but they are the samples for commonly asked questions.

This test aims to cover all topics which may appear on the actual test. However some topics may not be covered.

Studying this booklet will be preparing you for the actual test. It will not guarantee improving your test score but it will help you pass your exam on the first attempt.

**Some useful tips for answering multiple choice questions;**

- Start with the questions that you can easily answer.

- Underline the keywords in the question.

- Be sure to read all the choices given.

- Watch for keywords such as NOT, always, only, all, never, completely.

- Do not forget to answer every question.

**1**

Which of the following would be the best assistance the school becomes a resource to the community?

A) Parent resource center
B) School newsletters
C) Parent-teacher conferences
D) All of the above

**2**

**Speedread** is reading rapidly by assimilating several phrases or sentences at once.

What would be the general oral reading goal for fourth-graders in an elementary school?

A) 60-80 words per minute
B) 115-140 words per minute
C) 180-200 words per minute
D) 195-225 words per minute

**3**

Which of the following approaches should a teacher take to meet the developmental needs of all students in the class if she wants to incorporate art projects into the content areas for students who exhibit a wide range of fine motor skills?

A) Giving individual students access to specific art media based on their demonstrated skill levels
B) Allowing students to self-select from a variety of art media for each lesson
C) Using teacher-assigned art media for each individual lesson
D) Providing students with direct instruction in skills needed for proper use of various art media

**4**

Which of the following scientific term is used to refer a child's language development being delayed because of the environment?

A) The Teletubbies effect
B) Substantial lag
C) Psychosocial deprivation
D) Language deprivation disorder

CONTINUE ▶

Ms. Goodman wants to teach her Spanish-speaking fifth-grade students the vocabulary term "lunar phases" while exploring the lesson about the moon.

Which teaching approaches below can best help Ms. Goodman to teach the vocabulary term?

A)  Tell the class that they are going to discuss "phases of the moon" or "lunar phases"

B)  Have students write repeatedly the term "lunar phases" with corresponding drawings

C)  Sing a song whose lyrics have terms for the different lunar phases

D)  Write on the board the Spanish words "phase lunar" and its English equivalent "lunar phase" just below it to show their similarity

Mrs. Berckman, a fourth grade ENL teacher, has a newcomer student from a school in Honduras. It's the first time for the student to study in the U.S. Hence Mrs. Berckman finds it essential to assess the student's academic knowledge and skills.

What assessment should Mrs. Berckman use to yield the most useful information about the student's academic background?

A)  An English proficiency test

B)  An English norm-referenced battery of subject-area test

C)  A Spanish proficiency test

D)  A Spanish norm-referenced battery of subject-area test

**7**

Which of the terms below is illustrated when the students are exposed first to information about a subject matter before reading about it?

A)  Introducing background information reading technique

B)  Exploring the unknown reading technique

C)  Exposure to pre-reading concepts reading technique

D)  Wasting time reading technique

**8**

Which of the following activities would a student completing kindergarten demonstrate mastery in effective communication using organization skills?

A)  Sequencing events and using a story map when retelling a story

B)  Describing a favorite character from a book using complete sentences

C)  Performing short rhymes and plays for an audience of older students

D)  Identifying and pointing to letters of the alphabet in order

**9**

**The alphabetic principle** is the understanding that letters represent sounds which form words. It is the knowledge of predictable relationships between written letters and spoken sounds.

What does the alphabetic principle describe?

A)  The knowledge of letters and their shape

B)  The knowledge of vocabulary

C)  The relationship of letters and sound

D)  The relationship of vocabulary and letters

**10**

**Repeated reading** is an academic practice that aims to increase oral reading fluency. How many words are good for repeated reading experiences?

A)  100-150

B)  50-75

C)  50-200

D)  20-50

**11**

Which of the following terms is not defined correctly?

A) Development is the continuous process of change that all humans experience during their life.

B) Learning is the change of behaviors, thoughts or emotions based on genetics.

C) Growth is the physical process of development.

D) Maturation is the physical, emotional or intellectual process of development.

**12**

A parent confides to a teacher that they are deeply in debt and near eviction from their home during a parent-teacher conference.

Which of the following actions would be the teacher's most appropriate initial response?

A) Asking support for the family from the parents of other students in the class

B) Discussing the problem with the student's other teachers

C) Asking the parents' permission to share the information with school officials

D) Talking privately with the school principal about the matter

**13**

At the preselected stopping points, students refine, revise, and verify their predictions about what they read.

Which of the following strategies use stopping points to check for thinking processes during reading?

A) Predicting

B) Think-aloud

C) Skimming and scanning

D) Summarizing

**14**

A teacher wants to distribute parents with progress reports that are as significant as possible in describing their children's academic growth.

Which of the following practices would best achieve this goal?

A) Providing a glossary of assessment terminology with every progress report

B) Ensuring that each progress report includes test scores or detailed report

C) Writing the progress reports using straightforward language that is free of educational jargon

D) Including a copy of the teacher's grading policies with each progress report

**15**

During the concrete operational stage of cognitive development which of the following children are most likely to begin demonstrating?

A) Analyzing their thought
B) Solving a given problem in different ways
C) Thinking through a series of steps logically
D) Making specific observations to understand basic principles

**16**

Which of the following terms mean thinking and learning about one's own thinking processes?

A) Assimilation
B) Accommodation
C) Metacognition
D) Regulation of cognition

**17**

Which type of performance assessment lets the teacher decide what the students are able to do for long periods of time?

A) Extended performance assessment
B) Individual performance assessment
C) Restricted-response performance assessment
D) Authentic performance assessment

**18**

Which of the following statements is true?

A) Children's literature is often based directly on adult literature.
B) Many children's stories are derived from fairy tales and are, therefore, not very useful for modern life.
C) Many children's stories are derived from the oral tradition and, therefore, have origins that are difficult to trace.
D) All of the answers are true.

**19**

Which of the following is the best description of the primary role of a general education teacher in the execution of a student's Individualized Education Plan (IEP)?

A) Adjusting IEP goals periodically based on the student's strengths and needs

B) Scheduling support and related services required by the student's IEP

C) Modifying curriculum and instruction to support the student's IEP goals

D) Collecting evidence of compliance with modifications required by the student's IEP

**20**

**Creativity development** is a nonlinear and multifaceted process starting early in life.

Which of the following about creativity development and intelligence of a child is not correct?

A) Sternberg proposed The Triarchic Theory

B) Child's creativity can be assessed by The Torrance Test

C) Adoption studies show evidence of a genetic influence on intelligence

D) Crystallized intelligence refers to the knowledge that remains stable over the years.

**21**

Four-year-old Ken writes the letter K all around the edges of a card, with the picture of a dog image, and says, "This is my doggy. It says Floppy."

According to this, which of the following did Ken understand?

A) The function of print

B) The alphabetic knowledge

C) Hand and eye coordination

D) How words are decrypted

**22**

**Asperger Syndrome (AS)** is a neurobiological disorder on the higher-functioning end of the autism spectrum.

Which of the following is characteristic of a child with Asperger's Syndrome?

A) The difficulty with social interactions such as speaking and forming complete sentences

B) High academic performance and cognitive development

C) Inability to acquire new information in classes such as mathematics

D) Delayed mental development and motor skills development

**23**

Which of the following defines the role of a teacher in a student-centered environment?

A) Law enforcer who makes sure students are following the rules and regulations.

B) Co-teacher who works alongside the students to deliver lessons.

C) The organizer who monitors and supports student activities.

D) The dictator who tells students what to do and controls all their actions.

**24**

How would encouraging children to pretend-read to toys and stuffed animals while looking at books help support the children's early reading development?

A) By increasing awareness of the structure of words

B) By fostering concepts of print

C) By building knowledge of letter-sound relationships

D) By expanding oral vocabulary

**25**

Every week, a teacher sends students home with an envelope containing samples of their work and any necessary notices. The parents review the materials and sign and date the envelope, which the students return to the teacher the next day.

Which of the following is the primary benefit of this practice?

A) It increases parents' interest in their child's school experiences.

B) It helps the teacher maintain ongoing communication with parents.

C) It requires students to communicate with their parents about the school.

D) It reduces the teacher's need for formal conferences with parents.

**26**

Which of the following is not a correct explanation?

A) Metacognition means thinking and learning about one's own thinking and learning processes.

B) The schema is a term used by Piaget referring to a mental construct that one forms to understand the environment.

C) Assimilation happens when the existing schema needs to be modified to take in new information.

D) Self-efficacy is a term used by Bandura for self-confidence in one's ability to complete a specific task.

**CONTINUE ▶**

**27**

What was Eli M. Bower's contribution to the study of the education of children?

A)  He was the first researcher to clearly define high-functioning autism

B)  He conducted pioneering research on deficits in social imagination among children with Asperger's

C)  The discovery of autism and advocating for research on treatment options

D)  Pioneering researcher on Cognitive Disorder

**28**

What should teachers keep in mind when designing instruction?

A)  Not all kids are on the same level

B)  Instructional planning isn't as crucial as it is believed

C)  All students understand the same way

D)  The previous experiences of students aren't the base of learning

**29**

A team of science teachers meets regularly to review the scope of the content across grade levels.

Which of the following is the major benefit of this practice?

A)  It ensures the overall continuity of the math curriculum and skill instruction.

B)  It promotes flexible instructional pacing for math content and skills.

C)  It addresses the individual learning needs of students at varying developmental stages.

D)  It streamlines the process of curriculum planning and evaluation.

**30**

Which of the following about intelligence and creativity development of a child is not correct?

A)  The Theory of Multiple Intelligences was proposed by Gardner.

B)  Intelligence remains stable but IQ scores drop with age.

C)  The Fagan test evaluates an infant's intelligence through her socio-motor skills.

D)  IQ scores fluctuate during adolescence.

**31**

You are given the following sentence. How many of the words contain letters that seem to appear more than once in that word?

Going to a party alone can be an awkward social experience, but only if you let it become one.

A) 4

B) 5

C) 6

D) None of the above

**32**

Which of the following is not considered as a use of standardized assessments?

A) To evaluate whether students have learned what they are expected to learn

B) To determine whether educational policies are working as intended

C) To identify gaps in student learning and academic progress

D) To use standardized test results to alter classroom curriculum

**33**

**Guided reading** is an instructional approach that involves a teacher working with a small group of students who demonstrate similar reading behaviors and can all read similar levels of texts. The text is easy enough for students to read with teacher's skillful support.

What is the primary purpose of guided reading?

A) It helps students develop a deeper understanding of literature.

B) It helps students develop their oral reading skills.

C) It improves students' phonological awareness.

D) It expands students' reading power to increasingly difficult texts.

The teacher offers the word "stay", and the students brainstorm the words "postpone, delay, defer, put back, etc". Then the students play a game of charades in which individual students act out one of the descriptive verbs while the rest of the class tries to guess which verb it is.

In designing this lesson, the teacher most likely focused on the principle that learning is enhanced by the instruction that;

A) helps students recognize the relevance of new learning to their own lives and needs.

B) provides students with opportunities for active engagement in the learning process.

C) links new learning to students' prior knowledge and experience.

D) promotes students' view of learning as a challenging experience.

A second-grade teacher presents a lesson about short vowels. The teacher writes "_on" on the board, and asks students to suggest letters to put in the blank. Each time the students suggest a letter the teacher fills in the blank to form a new word and asks the class to read the word aloud.

Which of the following additional activities is most likely to address the developmental levels of all students in the class?

A) Allowing students to make sentences using the new words

B) Requesting from students to spell the new words aloud several times

C) Having students copy the list of new words into their writing journals

D) Giving students with cut-out letters to build more new words

**36**

By which of the following can teachers support student reading?

A)  Making students go over passages multiple times

B)  Using graphic organizers or visual aids during reading

C)  Offering rewards to the best reader

D)  Engaging in Round Robin reading to keep students on track

**37**

**Backward Design** is a method of designing educational curriculum by setting goals before choosing instructional methods and forms of assessment.

In curriculum planning according to backward design principles, which one below is correct?

A)  Design the end of the day before designing the beginning of the day

B)  Think of the big questions in a unit before the daily activities

C)  Start with plans for Friday and work backward to Monday

D)  Work on curriculum plans for June and move backward to September

**38**

A teacher wishes to use scaffolding to boost student learning. Which of the following is the best example of this strategy?

A)  Giving students charts labeled with relevant variables so that they can record data they gather during classroom science experiments

B)  Prompting students to identify personal goals that they hope to achieve

C)  Holding weekly geography bees with students to review important information covered during recent lessons

D)  Marking errors in students' descriptive paragraphs and asking them to rewrite the paragraphs correctly

**39**

Freud (1905) proposed that psychological development in childhood takes place in a series of fixed stages.

According to Freud's Psychosexual Development Theory, which of the following stages is associated with elementary school ages?

A)  The Latency stage

B)  The Genital stage

C)  The Oral stage

D)  The Phallic stage

CONTINUE ▶

Vygotsky is an educational psychologist who is well known for his sociocultural theory. According to this theory, social interaction leads to continuous step-by-step changes in children's thought and behavior that can vary greatly from culture to culture.

Which of the following about cognitive development and Vygotsky's theory is not correct?

A) Vygotsky used a sociocultural perspective in his theory of cognitive development.

B) Staying cognitively active is helpful for maintaining both fluid and crystallized intelligence.

C) According to Vygotsky, scaffolding is the process of constructing an internal representation of external physical objects or actions.

D) Lev Vygotsky is most well-known for a cultural-historical theory of cognitive development emphasizing social interactions and culture.

**Curriculum design** is a statement which identifies the elements of the curriculum, shows what their relationships are to each other. It also indicates the principles and the requirements of organization for the administrative conditions under which it is to operate.

Which of the following about curriculum design is not correct?

A) The curriculum is the stuff teachers teach

B) Curriculum models provide a framework for curriculum guides

C) Backward design in curriculum planning is designing the end of the day before designing the beginning of the day

D) Curriculum planning helps make sure teaching on a daily basis has a larger purpose

**42**

Subtracting three-digit numbers with regrouping has been completed in an elementary school class. Unit test results indicate that the majority of the students have not learned this concept well.

Which of the following would be appropriate in responding to this situation?

A) Reteach the topic so that students can master the concept

B) Ask students who mastered the concept to assist others with a supplemental assignment on the concept

C) Analyze students' scores and go over specific problem areas

D) Assign extra homework about the students' problem areas

**43**

(1) The officer asked the inmate if something was keeping him up at night.

(2) While supervising inmates working in the facility library, an officer noticed Inmate Y was having trouble staying awake while sorting books.

(3) The officer documented what Inmate Y told him and informed the housing unit supervisor of the situation.

(4) Inmate Y replied that he and his roommate, Inmate C, were not getting along and he was worried that Inmate C might try to attack him in his sleep.

(5) Later that day, both Inmate Y and Inmate C were taken to separate holding areas for questioning.

Which of the following choices represents the most logical order for the sentences given above?

A) 2, 1, 4, 3, 5

B) 3, 2, 1, 4, 5

C) 3, 1, 5, 4, 2

D) 2, 4, 3, 5, 1

44

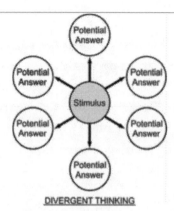

DIVERGENT THINKING

**Divergent thinking** is a thought process or method used to generate creative ideas by exploring many possible solutions. It typically occurs in a spontaneous, free-flowing, 'non-linear' manner, such that many ideas are generated in an emergent cognitive fashion.

Students in an early elementary class are completing a unit about their community. Which of the following teacher questions related to the unit would best promote the students' use of divergent thinking?

A) What was one important thing you learned about your community during the unit?

B) What are some things you can do on your own to keep your community clean and attractive?

C) What do police officers do to keep people in your community safe?

D) What do people use your community's public library for?

# SECTION 1

| # | Answer | Topic | Subtopic | # | Answer | Topic | Subtopic | # | Answer | Topic | Subtopic | # | Answer | Topic | Subtopic |
|---|--------|-------|----------|---|--------|-------|----------|---|--------|-------|----------|---|--------|-------|----------|
| 1 | A | TB | SB3 | 12 | C | TB | SB3 | 23 | C | TB | SB1 | 34 | C | TA | SA3 |
| 2 | B | TA | SA3 | 13 | B | TB | SB1 | 24 | B | TD | SD1 | 35 | D | TA | SA1 |
| 3 | B | TA | SA1 | 14 | C | TB | SB3 | 25 | B | TB | SB3 | 36 | D | TD | SD1 |
| 4 | C | TB | SB1 | 15 | C | TC | SC1 | 26 | C | TC | SC1 | 37 | B | TA | SA3 |
| 5 | D | TB | SB1 | 16 | C | TC | SC2 | 27 | B | TC | SC2 | 38 | A | TC | SC2 |
| 6 | D | TB | SB1 | 17 | A | TA | SA2 | 28 | A | TA | SA3 | 39 | A | TC | SC1 |
| 7 | A | TD | SD1 | 18 | C | TD | SD1 | 29 | A | TB | SB3 | 40 | C | TC | SC1 |
| 8 | A | TD | SD1 | 19 | C | TB | SB2 | 30 | C | TC | SC1 | 41 | C | TA | SA3 |
| 9 | C | TD | SD1 | 20 | D | TC | SC1 | 31 | D | TD | SD2 | 42 | A | TA | SA1 |
| 10 | C | TD | SD1 | 21 | A | TD | SD1 | 32 | D | TA | SA2 | 43 | C | TD | SD2 |
| 11 | B | TC | SC1 | 22 | A | TC | SC1 | 33 | D | TD | SD1 | 44 | B | TA | SA1 |

# Topics & Subtopics

| Code | Description | Code | Description |
|------|-------------|------|-------------|
| SA1 | Instruction | SC2 | Learning |
| SA2 | Assessment | SD1 | Reading Comprehension |
| SA3 | Curriculum | SD2 | Language Development |
| SB1 | Instructional Strategies | TA | Learning Environment |
| SB2 | Professional Development | TB | Professional Environment |
| SB3 | Communication | TC | Child Development & Learning |
| SC1 | Development | TD | Language & Literacy Development |

CONTINUE ▶

# TEST DIRECTION

DIRECTIONS

Read the questions carefully and then choose the ONE best answer to each question.

Be sure to allocate your time carefully so you are able to complete the entire test within the testing session. You may go back and review your answers at any time.

You may use any available space in your test booklet for scratch work.

Questions in this booklet are not actual test questions but they are the samples for commonly asked questions.

This test aims to cover all topics which may appear on the actual test. However some topics may not be covered.

Studying this booklet will be preparing you for the actual test. It will not guarantee improving your test score but it will help you pass your exam on the first attempt.

**Some useful tips for answering multiple choice questions;**

- Start with the questions that you can easily answer.

- Underline the keywords in the question.

- Be sure to read all the choices given.

- Watch for keywords such as NOT, always, only, all, never, completely.

- Do not forget to answer every question.

CONTINUE ▶

**1**

Which of the following practices does not contribute to language development?

A) Using rules, patterns, and conventions in teaching language

B) Changing the difficulty and breadth of reading materials

C) Using one-dimensional teaching approach

D) Seeking opportunities to develop language ability even beyond formal schooling

**2**

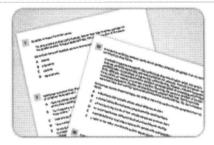

For which of the following asking questions at the end of a reading selection or unit is most appropriate?

A) When you want to clarify specific ideas for creative writing, journal writing, or group projects

B) When you need to review games, like acting out scenes in groups

C) When you want your students to have a game where they use questions to quiz one another

D) When you want to assess students' understanding of a reading selection

**3**

Reading is a complicated process which requires mastery of foundational reading skills.

Which of the following activities can be used to help younger readers develop necessary skills?

A) Sentence creation using sight words

B) Reading to a stuffed animal

C) Reviewing sight words

D) All of the above

**4**

Punctuation is used to create sense, clarity, and stress in sentences. Which of the below phrases has the correct punctuation?

A) Her moms car

B) Her mom"s car

C) Her mom's car

D) Her mom's car'

CONTINUE ▶

**5**

After John had drilled eight holes, he noticed that the edge of the wood was cracked.

What sentence type is illustrated by the sentence above?

A) Simple

B) Compound

C) Complex

D) Compound-complex

**6**

Which of the following is the most common during early childhood?

A) Independent reading

B) Learning by doing

C) Learning by playing

D) Direct instruction

**7**

Which of the following defines reading comprehension best?

A) Be able to read faster

B) Writing a story about what you read

C) Ability to read text, process it, and understand its meaning

D) None of the above

**8**

A student with cerebral palsy finishes an assignment. While watching him, an elementary art teacher notices that the student is having difficulty using specific art materials.

Which of the following is the most appropriate for the teacher to address special needs of this student?

A) Providing the student with a range of material alternatives

B) Sharing observations with the student's occupational therapist

C) Assigning the student a different art project

D) To find materials the student can easily manipulate.

**9**

David Perkins, a supporter of Gardner's theory of multiple intelligences, examined a large number of research studies both on the measurement of IQ and of programs of study designed to increase IQ.

According to Perkins intelligence has three dimensions? Which of the following gives these components?

A) Reflective, Neural and Experiential

B) Neural, Experiential and Emotional

C) Neural, Emotional and Experiential

D) Emotional, Experiential and Reflective

**10**

Which of the following defines a type of testing that regularly assesses students for systematic change or improvement?

A) Achievement test

B) Internal testing

C) Interim assessment

D) Dynamic assessment

**11**

Teachers often have the different level of students in the classroom. To meet the needs of all students, what should teachers do?

A) Provide different instructions.

B) Continue to teach according to the unit and lesson plans.

C) Teach grade level standards only.

D) Expect students to follow along, regardless of skill level.

**12**

**An inference** is an educated guess that's drawn from evidence and reasoning. Making an inference is a result of a process which requires reading a text, noting specific details, and then putting those details together to achieve a new understanding.

In drawing an inference from a text they have previously read, what is the first step readers must take?

A) Look for clues in the text

B) Put the pieces together in a logical way to produce a reasonable conclusion

C) Think about what they already know from their own experience in the real world

D) None of the above

CONTINUE ▶

The teacher instructs students to include drafts as well as final versions of the writing samples in their working portfolio.

Which of the following is a primary benefit of using this type of portfolio with students?

A) It documents students' learning abilities over time.

B) It interprets one student's performance about other students.

C) It provides a reliable means of predicting students' future performances.

D) It enables the teacher to determine students' mastery of large domains of content.

After teaching a lesson on persuasive writing, a fourth-grade teacher involves students in a brainstorming activity to identify a topic they would like to write about. The students decide to write an essay to the school board about the School Bus policy.

Which of the following is the most significant benefit of including the brainstorming activity in this lesson?

A) To increase the level of engagement among students having a difficult time mastering persuasive writing.

B) To connect persuasive writing skills to an issue that students find personally meaningful.

C) To give students an opportunity to practice persuasive writing in a content area context.

D) To help students understand the relationship between creative thinking and persuasive writing.

**15**

Which of the following defines validity?

A) The degree to which an assessment tool produces stable and consistent results

B) The extent to which a test (such as a chemical, physical, or scholastic test) accurately measures what it is supposed to measure

C) The extent to which an assessment measures the achievement of desired objectives

D) The extent to which an assessment covers all the items that have been taught or studied.

**16**

If atoms are the letters of the chemical language, then molecules are the words. But to put the chemical letters together to form chemical words, we have to know something about the rules of chemical spelling.

The discussion of atoms is introduced in the passage above by using which technique?

A) An analogy

B) An aphorism

C) An example

D) A hypothesis

**17**

A teacher is visiting a local business with a student. When the student does not understand an unknown word, "co-working space," the teacher breaks it into parts, so it is easy for the student to understand and has the student determine the meaning of "co" and the meaning of "working"

The activity deals with the knowledge of which of the following language concepts?

A) Morphemes

B) Orthography

C) Phonemes

D) None of them

**18**

Which of the following about intelligence and creativity development of a child is not correct?

A) The first IQ test was developed by Alfred Binet.

B) A score of 120 on the IQ test is a low IQ.

C) Identical twins raised together have IQ scores that are more similar than identical twins raised apart.

D) Myelination is the process of developing white matter covering on nerve cells.

**19**

Which of the following explains why using essay tests to evaluate student learning is an essential challenge for teachers?

A) They are not useful in assessing specific kinds of thinking skills.

B) They tend to promote guessing in student answers.

C) They have a tendency to be hard to adjust to instructional objectives.

D) They are hard to score objectively and fairly.

**20**

Which of the following about Observations and Inferences is not correct?

A) Observations are mere generalizations; inferences are eye-witness accounts.

B) Observations are based on information seen; inferences are based on data already known.

C) Observations may skew the truth; inferences reveal the actual state regardless of speaker's claims.

D) All of these answers are correct.

**21**

Which of the following does differentiating instruction mean?

A) The use of different instructional strategies to support all students

B) The use of different curriculum just for ELL students

C) The use of different teachers to teach lessons in the classroom

D) Asking teachers to deliver instruction in multiple languages

**22**

Which of the following characterizes the cognitive development of 4-year-old children according to the typical sequence of human development?

A) Understanding cause-effect relationships via Hypothetical thinking

B) Learning via direct and immediate sensory stimuli

C) Using logic to solve some problems

D) Egocentric thinking of the situations based mainly on their appearance.

Which of the following about basic terms of development is not correct?

A) Nurture refers to the effect of the environment upon a person.

B) Nature refers to the traits that are inherited.

C) Maturation is limitless, but Growth is limited.

D) Learning new skills is an example of growth.

Educational measurement refers to the use of educational assessments and the analysis of data to infer the abilities and proficiencies of students.

Which of the following about measurement is not true?

A) The most significant quality of a proper assessment is validity.

B) An assessment is the process of gathering and discussing information from multiple and diverse sources to develop a deep understanding of what students know, understand, and can do with their knowledge as a result of their educational experiences.

C) A standardized test is any form of test that requires all test takers to answer the same questions or a selection of items from the standard bank of questions.

D) While interpreting raw scores, knowledge of basic statistics is essential.

**25**

**Curriculum guides** are documents used by states, school districts and individual schools to guide teachers in their instruction. Many guides are detailed, giving teachers a specific scope of what to teach and when. Many provide additional resources, such as necessary materials and assessment tools.

Which of the following about curriculum guides is not correct?

A) It helps teachers decide what to teach and when.

B) It can be based on grade level of students.

C) It can not be based on the number of students in each class.

D) It helps teachers decide on classroom management strategies.

**26**

Regarding the social development of nine-year-old students, which of the following teaching strategies is likely to have the most positive influence?

A) Emphasizing student-led activities

B) Encouraging students during challenging activities

C) Giving a chance for students to express their feelings freely in the classroom

D) Assigning cooperative rather than competitive student activities

**27**

Student-centered learning is also known as learner-centered education. In student-centered learning, methods of teaching shift the focus of instruction from the teacher to the student so that students move from passive receivers of information to active participants in their own discovery process.

Which of the following defines the role of a teacher in a student-centered environment?

A) Law enforcer who makes sure students are following the rules and regulations.

B) Co-teacher who works alongside the students to deliver lessons.

C) The organizer who monitors and supports student activities.

D) A dictator who tells students what to do and controls all their actions.

**28**

Which of the following learning opportunities is most likely to promote the development of initiative in kindergarten students?

A) Providing students with charts to self-monitor their progress

B) Assigning responsibility for selected classroom tasks to students

C) Giving students ongoing feedback about their progress

D) Encouraging students to self-select center time activities

CONTINUE ▶

**29**

Which of the following is not an essential piece of guided reading?

A) Use of texts that challenge students' current reading levels.

B) It helps students to become independent readers.

C) Teaching students various strategies used in reading.

D) Students are grouped according to their reading ability.

**30**

**The curriculum** can be defined as the totality of student experiences that occur in the educational process.

Which of the following about curriculum is not correct?

A) Curriculum planning is crucial because it makes classroom discipline easier.

B) A curriculum map is an ever-evolving document that should generally be followed based on the needs of the students.

C) Big ideas are essential in curriculum planning because it helps the teacher figure out what's most important about a curriculum.

D) Modern curriculum models are often a blend of process and product.

**31**

**A chapbook** is an early type of popular literature printed in early modern Europe. Chapbooks were commonly small, paper-covered booklets which was produced cheaply.

According to the definition given above, which of the following about chapbook is true?

A) A child could easily understand it

B) It did not have any more than 40 pages

C) Very cheap so that layperson could easily buy

D) All of the above

**32**

An early childhood teacher holds regular class meetings and begins these meetings by giving individual students an opportunity to recognize the efforts or achievement of a classmate or to thank a classmate for assistance with a difficult or challenging task.

Beginning class meetings in this way are most likely to have which of the following outcomes?

A) Creating a learning environment that fosters excellence

B) Building a supportive and caring classroom community

C) Promoting students' self-monitoring of their behavior

D) Communicating with students high expectations for their learning

**33**

Which type of performance assessment lets the teacher decide what the students can do for long periods of time?

A) Extended performance assessment

B) Individual performance assessment

C) Restricted-response performance assessment

D) Authentic performance assessment

**34**

An effective teacher engages all students and provides a learning environment where all students can learn.

Which of the following is a strategy used in effective teaching?

A) Breaking complex material down and making complicated topics easy to understand

B) Getting feedback from students and motivating them

C) Promoting student interest and giving plenty of examples to clarify the topic

D) All of the above

**35**

Which of the following about development is not correct?

A) B.F. Skinner has contributed to the behaviorist perspective of Educational Psychology.

B) Learning how to do addition is an example of cognitive development.

C) Environment influences a person's genes. This belief is an example of the interaction of DNA and heredity.

D) Emotional development is about understanding emotions while social development is about learning to interact with others.

**36**

It is a narrative that takes abstract ideas of behavior, such as good or bad, wise or foolish, and attempts to make them concrete and striking. Aside from this, the main character in this type of narrative is usually an animal or an inanimate object that behaves like a human and engages in a single significant act that is intended to teach a moral lesson.

What is the name of this type of narrative?

A) A myth

B) A fable

C) An epic

D) A legend

**Gestalt Psychology** is a movement in psychology founded in Germany in 1912, seeking to explain perceptions regarding gestalt's rather than by analyzing their constituent's and an attempt to understand the laws behind the ability to acquire and maintain meaningful understandings in a chaotic world.

Which of the following statements would be in agreement with Gestalt theory?

A) Single notes must remain constant to recognize an overall melody.

B) Pieces of a puzzle take priority over the total image.

C) Perceptual experience is more than the sum of its elements.

D) Slower the image projection faster the perception of movement.

**Educational Psychology** is the study of how humans learn and retain knowledge, primarily in educational settings like classrooms. It includes social, emotional and cognitive learning processes.

Which of the following about Educational Psychology is not correct?

A) The responsibility of learning falls on the learner rather than the teacher according to the Constructivist perspective.

B) Albert Bandura contributed a lot to the Social-Cognitive Educational Psychology.

C) Learning occurs through stage-like processes according to the Developmental Educational Psychology.

D) Learning occurs through observation according to the Cognitive Educational Psychology.

**39**

For a gravity science experiment; students drop two pieces of paper, one flat and one that has been collapsed into a ball, from a height of 7 feet. They observe which piece of paper hits the ground first. As a follow-up activity, the teacher has small groups discuss the results of this experiment.

Which of the following discussion questions would most efficiently prompt students to use reasoning skills to conclude from the experiment?

A) What would happen if one piece of paper weighed more than the other?

B) Is the same amount of gravity exerted on both pieces of paper?

C) What would happen if a different kind of paper were used?

D) Why did one piece of paper fall faster than the other?

**40**

A third-grade class is about to begin reading a new chapter in their science textbook. Which of the following would be the most effective way for the teacher to promote students' comprehension when they begin reading?

A) Having students skim the chapter, write down any unfamiliar words, and look up the words in a dictionary

B) Assigning students to small groups in which the members take turns reading sections of the text out loud

C) Holding a brief discussion of the word identification strategies the class has learned and listing the strategy on the board

D) Helping the class generate a chart of what they know about the subject and what they would like to learn

Which of the following about sensory and perceptional development is not correct?

A) Sensory perception is defined as the change in sensation that we experience with age.

B) The categories of sensitive periods are; language, order, sensory skills, motor skills and social skills.

C) The term "sensitive periods" is associated with Maria Montesorri and Hugo de Vries.

D) A condition where a person receives little or no sensory input is called as sensory deprivation.

Which of the following strategies would help lessen the language demand for a fourth-grade ENL student who is struggling to read and comprehend while building background knowledge so that she can experience more considerable success in her social studies class?

A) Designating a peer who is a native speaker of English with strong reading skills to read the text out loud to the student.

B) Providing the student with a graphic organizer, such as a five senses chart, to complete while reading the text.

C) Assigning supplemental reading to the student that relates to the text, such as a magazine or newspaper article.

D) Providing the student with a chapter summary in simplified English for reading at home the day before introducing a new chapter in class.

**43**

**Cognitive development** is the construction of thought processes, including remembering, problem-solving, and decision-making from childhood through adolescence to adulthood.

Which of the following about cognitive development is not correct?

A) Knowing the number of days in a year is an example of crystallized intelligence.

B) Memory loss and Dementia is a symptom of Alzheimer's disease.

C) Remembering a password to enter into a website is an example of using short-term memory.

D) An individual's attention span typically decreases through adolescence and childhood.

**44**

If a student is interested in a subject, but the school does not offer any classes in it, in which way the student can acquire skills in this subject?

A) Reading books about the subject will enable the student to acquire desired skills.

B) He can not enroll in an outside course to learn because he is already enrolled in high school.

C) An internship or apprenticeship will provide instruction, modeling, and hands-on learning by doing.

D) He can find YouTube videos teaching the skills but not further reading/study matter.

CONTINUE ▶

# SECTION 2

| # | Answer | Topic | Subtopic | | # | Answer | Topic | Subtopic | | # | Answer | Topic | Subtopic | | # | Answer | Topic | Subtopic |
|---|--------|-------|----------|---|---|--------|-------|----------|---|---|--------|-------|----------|---|---|--------|-------|----------|
| 1 | C | TB | SB1 | | 12 | A | TD | SD1 | | 23 | D | TC | SC1 | | 34 | D | TB | SB1 |
| 2 | B | TD | SD1 | | 13 | A | TA | SA3 | | 24 | D | TA | SA2 | | 35 | C | TC | SC1 |
| 3 | D | TD | SD1 | | 14 | B | TA | SA3 | | 25 | D | TA | SA3 | | 36 | B | TD | SD1 |
| 4 | C | TD | SD2 | | 15 | B | TA | SA2 | | 26 | D | TC | SC1 | | 37 | C | TA | SA1 |
| 5 | C | TD | SD1 | | 16 | A | TD | SD1 | | 27 | C | TC | SC2 | | 38 | D | TC | SC1 |
| 6 | C | TC | SC2 | | 17 | A | TB | SB1 | | 28 | D | TB | SB1 | | 39 | D | TB | SB2 |
| 7 | C | TD | SD1 | | 18 | B | TC | SC1 | | 29 | A | TD | SD1 | | 40 | D | TD | SD1 |
| 8 | B | TC | SC1 | | 19 | D | TB | SB1 | | 30 | A | TA | SA3 | | 41 | A | TC | SC1 |
| 9 | A | TA | SA1 | | 20 | B | TB | SB3 | | 31 | D | TD | SD1 | | 42 | D | TD | SD1 |
| 10 | D | TA | SA2 | | 21 | A | TB | SB2 | | 32 | B | TA | SA1 | | 43 | D | TC | SC1 |
| 11 | B | TA | SA3 | | 22 | D | TC | SC1 | | 33 | A | TB | SB1 | | 44 | A | TA | SA3 |

# Topics & Subtopics

| Code | Description | | Code | Description |
|------|-------------|---|------|-------------|
| SA1 | Instruction | | SC2 | Learning |
| SA2 | Assessment | | SD1 | Reading Comprehension |
| SA3 | Curriculum | | SD2 | Language Development |
| SB1 | Instructional Strategies | | TA | Learning Environment |
| SB2 | Professional Development | | TB | Professional Environment |
| SB3 | Communication | | TC | Child Development & Learning |
| SC1 | Development | | TD | Language & Literacy Development |

CONTINUE ▶

# TEST DIRECTION

**DIRECTIONS**

Read the questions carefully and then choose the ONE best answer to each question.

Be sure to allocate your time carefully so you are able to complete the entire test within the testing session. You may go back and review your answers at any time.

You may use any available space in your test booklet for scratch work.

Questions in this booklet are not actual test questions but they are the samples for commonly asked questions.

This test aims to cover all topics which may appear on the actual test. However some topics may not be covered.

Studying this booklet will be preparing you for the actual test. It will not guarantee improving your test score but it will help you pass your exam on the first attempt.

**Some useful tips for answering multiple choice questions;**

- Start with the questions that you can easily answer.

- Underline the keywords in the question.

- Be sure to read all the choices given.

- Watch for keywords such as NOT, always, only, all, never, completely.

- Do not forget to answer every question.

**1**

Bomb > Explosion

Drinking > Intoxication

An analogy is a comparison of two things to show their similarities What type of analogy is used above?

A) Antonym
B) Part and whole
C) Classification
D) Cause and effect

**2**

"Adam likes gorgeous artwork, extravagant clothes, and immoderate cars. He is so frugal that he hangs cheap posters on his walls and drives an economy hatchback car."

Which of the following word best suits the examples of 'Cheap posters' and 'economy hatchback car' in the paragraph below?

A) Extravagant
B) Unbalanced
C) None of these
D) Frugal

**3**

What is the reason behind the impact of the quality of text on comprehension?

A) Lack of quality books limits student's ability to engage with the text.
B) Reading limited types of books limits exposure to genres.
C) Limited access to books eliminates topics some students find entertaining.
D) All of these are true.

**4**

In what way can non-native English learners be taught the English alphabet?

A) Through teaching them which letters are similar and which are not
B) Through building their English words vocabulary
C) Through teaching them the different letter sounds
D) All of the above

**5**

Which of the following about reading instruction is true?

A) The importance of reading books and phonics are the same.
B) Phonics is more important than reading.
C) Reading books is not essential.
D) Neither phonics or reading books is essential.

**6**

Which of the following defines Sensory perception?

A) The awareness of things with the senses
B) The degree we respond to a stimulus
C) The level of strength of perception
D) The improvement in the sensation that is experienced with age

    35     CONTINUE ▶

**7**

Which of the following is a carefully designed display recording the progress of children's projects and the process they employed during explorations?

A) A documentation panel

B) A KWHL chart

C) A concept map

D) A transcript

**8**

Which of the following are included in the steps that are used in learning to read?

A) Memorization of ABC's

B) Recognizing spoken words when written

C) Reading aloud

D) All of the above

**9**

Why is it essential for a speaker to make eye contact with members of the audience?

A) It tells the audience that he is confident in the material.

B) It tells the audience that he is dishonest.

C) It creates a bond of distrust.

D) It makes the audience less likely to remain engaged.

**10**

Out of the below lines of dialogue, which one has the correct punctuation?

A) "I went to the market" Jane said, "but I didn't find anything I wanted to buy."

B) "I went to the market," Jane said, "but I didn't find anything I wanted to buy."

C) "I went to the market," Jane said "but I didn't find anything I wanted to buy."

D) "I went to the market," Jane said, "But I didn't find anything I wanted to buy."

**11**

A teacher has implemented learning objectives for a unit of study. Which of the following steps should the teacher take next?

A) Put in order the activities to help students meet the learning objectives.

B) Implement strategies for presenting concepts related to the learning objectives.

C) Identify skills that students will need to develop in meeting the learning objectives.

D) Determine how to evaluate students' mastery of the learning objectives.

**12**

Which of the following approaches should a teacher take to meet the developmental needs of all students in the class if she wants to incorporate art projects into the content areas for students who exhibit a wide range of fine motor skills?

A) Giving individual students access to specific art media based on their demonstrated skill levels

B) Allowing students to self-select from a variety of art media for each lesson

C) Using teacher-assigned art media for each lesson

D) Providing students with direct instruction in skills needed for proper use of various art media

**13**

Which of the following shows the "average differences" from what most people score on a test?

A) Standard Deviation

B) Mean

C) Median

D) Mode

**14**

Sweet spot enhances the ability to learn fast. What is the sweet spot for learning, when the task is neither too hard nor too easy?

A) The sweet zone

B) Zone of beginning

C) Zone of learning

D) Zone of the proximal development

**15**

Literacy skills help students gain knowledge through reading. They include awareness of the sounds of language, awareness of print, and the relationship between letters and sounds. Other literacy skills include vocabulary, spelling, and comprehension.

Which of the following defines literacy skills?

A) It refers to the ways students interact with adults.

B) It is the ability to speak several languages.

C) It is the reasoning skills necessary to solve problems.

D) It is the knowledge and practices related reading and writing.

**16**

**Critical thinking** is disciplined thinking that is clear, rational, open-minded, and informed by evidence.

Which of the following is recommended during the critical thinking process?

A) Considering the consequences of your conclusion

B) Avoiding discussing the origins of your point of view

C) Avoiding focusing on statistical evidence since most people care more about personal stories

D) Judging all points of view as equally valid and acceptable

**17**

What are the benefits of reading?

A) Reading boosts your vocabulary

B) Reading keeps your brain young

C) Helps hand/eye coordination

D) All of the above

**18**

"The goal of summative assessment is to evaluate student learning at the end of an instructional unit by comparing it against some standard or benchmark. Summative assessments are often high stakes, which means that they have a high point value.

Which of the options given below can be considered as an example of a summative assessment?

A) A standardized state exam

B) Writing a journal

C) A quiz

D) A peer/ self-assessment

CONTINUE ▶

**19**

**Neurological disorders** are diseases of the brain, spine and the nerves that connect them. There are more than 600 diseases of the nervous system, such as brain tumors, epilepsy, and Parkinson's disease.

Which of the following neurological disorders may cause language delay?

A) Autism spectrum disorder

B) Developmental speech disorder

C) Cerebral palsy (CP)

D) All of the above

**20**

What should teachers keep in mind when designing instruction?

A) Not all kids are on the same level.

B) Instructional planning isn't as crucial as it is believed.

C) All students understand the same way.

D) The previous experiences of students aren't the base of learning.

**21**

When selecting reading materials to support the concepts presented in a lesson, a teacher should ask which of the following questions first?

A) Are these materials usable for more than one lesson presentation?

B) Will students require additional instruction to use these materials effectively?

C) Do these materials support a variety of student groupings?

D) Are these materials consistent with the students' comprehension and skill levels?

**22**

Which of the following actions should be done by teacher immediately after the students have finished reading?

A) Reading important parts again

B) Asking students to write the main idea

C) Basic comprehension

D) Group discussion about the passage that has been read in the class

When selecting reading materials to support the concepts presented in a lesson, a teacher should ask which of the following questions first?

A) Are these materials usable for more than one lesson presentation?

B) Will students require additional instruction to use these materials effectively?

C) Do these materials support a variety of student groupings?

D) Are these materials consistent with the students' comprehension and skill levels?

English-language learners, or ELLs, are students who are unable to communicate fluently or efficiently learn in English, who often come from non-English-speaking homes and backgrounds, and who typically require specialized or modified instructions.

What is the first way in which teachers can apply processes of acquiring and integrating new knowledge to help ELL students access meaningful learning?

A) Activate accommodation

B) Activate all at once

C) Activate assimilation

D) Activate prior knowledge

**25**

School district supplies teachers with curriculum and necessary documents. Why should teachers still prepare annual and unit plans?

A) It is not necessary to develop annual and unit plans.

B) All school districts force teachers to write and submit annual and unit plans.

C) While preparing annual and unit plans by their own, teachers better understand what to teach.

D) Textbooks may not address all required standards, and teachers might have to supplement the curriculum.

**26**

**The schema** is an abstract concept in cognitive development, which was first used by Piaget. He emphasized the importance of schemas and described how they were developed or acquired.

Which of the following defines schema best?

A) It is a cognitive framework or concept that helps organize and interpret information.

B) It defines the process of saving knowledge in the brain.

C) It refers to the first phase of cognitive development.

D) It is a term used to explain how the brain develops.

**27**

By the end of the first grade, which of the following most students will be able to do?

A) Notice and comment on aspects of the writer's craft.

B) Use reading as a tool for learning in content areas.

C) Sustain interest and understanding over long texts.

D) Use letter-sound information along with meaning and language to decode words.

**28**

Fine motor skills are achieved when children learn to use their smaller muscles, like muscles in the hands, fingers, and wrists.

In a third grade class, which of the below would be the teacher's best technique for encouraging the advancement of students fine motor skills?

A) Providing children with color pencils to allow them to trace the outlines of letters

B) Engaging children in activities such as doing finger plays and playing with blocks and beads

C) Involving children in drawing pictures

D) Involving children in singing song

**29**

**Communication** is exchanging information by speaking, writing, or using some other medium.

Which of the following is not correct about communication?

A) Nonverbal communication is the use of body movements to send a message.

B) If a speaker uses graphs, charts he is using an assertion of logic.

C) It is never appropriate to use obscene language in a speech.

D) Pitch has a psychological effect that influences how people perceive your speech's content.

**30**

**Scaffolding** refers to a variety of instructional techniques used to move students progressively toward stronger understanding and, in the end, higher independence in the learning process.

Which of the following is the advantage of Scaffolding instruction?

A) Track students so that the high-level students are in one group and the low-level students are in another.

B) Break instruction into smaller components so that students can organize information.

C) Water down the curriculum so that students can be successful even if it's at a lower level.

D) Cut out parts of the curriculum determined to be irrelevant.

**31**

Which of the following does a raw score represent?

A) A family of scores that allow us to make comparisons between test scores.

B) The average performance at age and grade levels.

C) How close to the average the student's score fall.

D) The number of items a student answers correctly without adjustment for guessing.

Sight words, often also called high-frequency sight words, are commonly used words that young children are encouraged to memorize. Sight words account for a large percentage (up to 75%) of the words used in beginning children's print materials.

If children recognize sight words automatically then they will be able to identify the majority of words in a beginning text before they even attempt to read it. It will allow the child to concentrate on meaning and comprehension as they read without having to stop and decode every single word.

Which of the following defines sight words?

A)  Basic words that have letters less than five

B)  Words that refer to the numbers

C)  Common words that can be memorized

D)  Words that draw a picture in a story

An elementary teacher notices that one of his students frequently appears drained and stated she had not received meals at home. The teacher is concerned that the student is being neglected.

Which of the following is the most appropriate action for the teacher to take concerning this student?

A)  Talk to the student's previous teachers to determine if they observed similar signs of neglect.

B)  Send home with the student a list of social service agencies that may be able to assist the family.

C)  Contact the parents or guardians to express his concerns.

D)  Report the suspected neglect following district guidelines.

A third-grade teacher is aware that students are often slow to make friends with new classmates. She wants to promote their acceptance of a student who will be joining the class.

By which of the following can the teacher best achieve this purpose?

A) Displaying exciting information about the new student on a class bulletin board.

B) Forming teams of students to assist the new student with various aspects of daily routines and activities.

C) Asking a student to interview the new student and share information about the new student with the class.

D) Assigning the new student to share a sought-after classroom job with a partner.

A kindergarten teacher makes display cards with the words I, me, and you. After introducing the cards to the class and reading them together, the teacher posts them on a word wall near the reading area. During the next week when reading a "big book" aloud to the class, the teacher occasionally pauses to point out one of the words on the page.

Which of the following ways would the activities stated above efficiently promote the students' reading development?

A) By providing them guided practice reading common word patterns

B) By promoting their use of contextual clues to identify words

C) By providing them explicit instruction in print concepts related to words

D) By promoting their recognition of high-frequency words by sight

Some students are making procedural errors in experimenting with the class. Which of the following actions would likely be the most effective for the teacher to take in response to this situation?

A) Talking about the procedures for the experiment before allowing students to continue

B) Having students write down the procedures before continuing the experiment

C) Modeling each step of the experiment and frequently checking for students' understanding

D) Having the students experiment one step at a time as it is explained

A second-grade teacher meets with the student's father. The student's grade equivalent score on a standardized math test is 5.5. Based on this score, the student's parents want the teacher to arrange for the student to receive math instruction with a fourth-grade class.

Which of the following is the most appropriate response for the teacher to make the father's request?

A) Agree to arrange for the student to attend fourth-grade math classes.

B) Suggest that they review the student's test scores in other subject areas to determine whether the student is eligible for grade acceleration.

C) Offer to provide the student with fourth-grade level independent learning opportunities in math.

D) Explain that the score indicates the student's level of performance on second-grade, rather than fourth-grade, level math.

A fourth-grade student with disabilities uses a communication board, and his family moves to a new community. Before the student's arrival in class, which of the following is most likely to assist students in making the new student a part of their classroom community?

A) Discussing with the class how the new student communicates and allowing students to try out a similar assistive technology device.

B) Arranging for a different member of the class to act as a buddy to the new student each day.

C) Having students take turns trying to communicate without using their voices and discussing how having this difficulty would affect them.

D) Having students brainstorm and discuss traits that make them different from their classmates.

Which of the following activities would more thoroughly foster a parent-teacher relationship to help students achieve their goals?

A) Asking parents to visit the classroom to observe tasks students are completing as well as to assist with class activities.

B) Encouraging parents to attend an event at a community facility that allows them to read and interact with their children using reading strategies learned in class.

C) Requiring parents to sign a weekly work folder contract stating they reviewed their children's completed work and helped them finish homework.

D) E-mailing parents weekly about student progress and recommending activities both in and out of school that would help meet their child's individual needs.

46                                CONTINUE ▶

Third-grade teacher Amanda is making plans to hold a parent conference with the parents in her class. During each meeting, Amanda will discuss broad goals and expectations for all students in the class.

Which of the following additional teacher actions during the conference would best help elevate positive association and a sense of partnership with parents?

A) Providing a thorough review of the second-grade curriculum in each subject and giving parents time to ask questions about the content to be covered.

B) Encouraging parents to share their own goals for their child's learning and development during the upcoming year as well as any concerns they may have.

C) Soliciting from parents information about any problematic situations in the home that they believe may affect their child's learning and achievement in the school.

D) Sharing information with parents about the teacher's own personal and educational background and his professional credentials

# SECTION 3

| #  | Answer | Topic | Subtopic | #  | Answer | Topic | Subtopic | #  | Answer | Topic | Subtopic | #  | Answer | Topic | Subtopic |
|----|--------|-------|----------|----|--------|-------|----------|----|--------|-------|----------|----|--------|-------|----------|
| 1  | D      | TD    | SD1      | 11 | C      | TA    | SA3      | 21 | D      | TA    | SA3      | 31 | D      | TA    | SA2      |
| 2  | D      | TD    | SD1      | 12 | B      | TA    | SA1      | 22 | C      | TD    | SD1      | 32 | C      | TD    | SD1      |
| 3  | D      | TD    | SD1      | 13 | A      | TA    | SA2      | 23 | D      | TD    | SD1      | 33 | D      | TB    | SB3      |
| 4  | D      | TB    | SB1      | 14 | D      | TB    | SB1      | 24 | D      | TA    | SA1      | 34 | B      | TB    | SB3      |
| 5  | A      | TD    | SD1      | 15 | D      | TB    | SB1      | 25 | D      | TA    | SA3      | 35 | D      | TD    | SD1      |
| 6  | A      | TC    | SC1      | 16 | C      | TB    | SB3      | 26 | A      | TB    | SB2      | 36 | C      | TA    | SA3      |
| 7  | A      | TA    | SA1      | 17 | A      | TD    | SD1      | 27 | D      | TA    | SA3      | 37 | D      | TB    | SB3      |
| 8  | B      | TD    | SD1      | 18 | A      | TA    | SA2      | 28 | B      | TD    | SD1      | 38 | A      | TB    | SB3      |
| 9  | A      | TB    | SB3      | 19 | D      | TB    | SB2      | 29 | D      | TB    | SB3      | 39 | B      | TB    | SB3      |
| 10 | B      | TD    | SD2      | 20 | A      | TB    | SB1      | 30 | B      | TA    | SA1      | 40 | A      | TB    | SB3      |

# Topics & Subtopics

| Code | Description               | Code | Description                    |
|------|---------------------------|------|--------------------------------|
| SA1  | Instruction               | SD1  | Reading Comprehension          |
| SA2  | Assessment                | SD2  | Language Development           |
| SA3  | Curriculum                | TA   | Learning Environment           |
| SB1  | Instructional Strategies  | TB   | Professional Environment       |
| SB2  | Professional Development  | TC   | Child Development & Learning   |
| SB3  | Communication             | TD   | Language & Literacy Development |
| SC1  | Development               |      |                                |

48

CONTINUE ▶

# TEST DIRECTION

**DIRECTIONS**

Read the questions carefully and then choose the ONE best answer to each question.

Be sure to allocate your time carefully so you are able to complete the entire test within the testing session. You may go back and review your answers at any time.

You may use any available space in your test booklet for scratch work.

Questions in this booklet are not actual test questions but they are the samples for commonly asked questions.

This test aims to cover all topics which may appear on the actual test. However some topics may not be covered.

Studying this booklet will be preparing you for the actual test. It will not guarantee improving your test score but it will help you pass your exam on the first attempt.

**Some useful tips for answering multiple choice questions;**

- Start with the questions that you can easily answer.

- Underline the keywords in the question.

- Be sure to read all the choices given.

- Watch for keywords such as NOT, always, only, all, never, completely.

- Do not forget to answer every question.

**1**

You are given the following sentence. Out of the options below, which one indicates best if there is an English grammar problem with it?

There is a loophole in the rules concerning academic progress that May allow a student to regain eligibility for financial aid by changing degree programs or by transferring to another college.

A) "eligibility" should be "elegibility"

B) "programs" should be "programms"

C) "May" should be "may"

D) There are no grammar problems

**2**

Which of the following reflects Bandura's point of view about learning?

A) It is not influenced by self-efficacy.

B) It can occur in the absence of a response.

C) It is facilitated by the unconscious mind.

D) It is not facilitated by reinforcement.

**3**

Which of the following zones is the slightest major area regarding reading comprehension abilities?

A) After reading zone

B) Before reading zone

C) Background reading zone

D) During reading zone

**4**

In the development of language, which of the following theories places the most emphasis on social interaction?

A) Constructivist

B) Humanist

C) Discovery Learning

D) Interactionist

**5**

Which of the following explains how a child learns to understand words?

A) How they are used
B) Who is saying them
C) What is going on when he hears them
D) All of the above

**6**

Which of the following practices does not contribute to language development?

A) Using rules, patterns, and conventions in teaching language
B) Changing the difficulty and breadth of reading materials
C) Using one-dimensional teaching approach
D) Seeking opportunities to develop language ability even beyond formal schooling.

**7**

A teacher wants to support vocabulary development for her English-language students.

Which approach should she use to help meet her goal?

A) Requiring students memorize a list of definitions and words weekly
B) Using engaging literature to introduce words in context to students
C) Introducing new words to the students at the beginning of every unit
D) Letting each student learn with a peer to discuss the definition of unfamiliar words

**8**

Reading fluency is very important for word recognition and comprehension. Which of the following is an example of reading fluency?

A) Reading loudly
B) Reading very quickly
C) Reading at a slow pace
D) Reading quickly and with expression

51                    **CONTINUE ▶**

**9**

What should teachers do to help their students identify the main points during a reading exercise?

A) Look for a standard or reoccurring theme

B) Count the events that take place

C) Rewrite the events in the story or text

D) Read the text without an opinion

**10**

The teacher instructs students to include drafts as well as final versions of the writing samples in their working portfolio.

Which of the following is a primary benefit of using this type of portfolio with students?

A) It documents students' learning abilities over time.

B) It interprets one student's performance about other students.

C) It provides a reliable means of predicting students' future performances.

D) It enables the teacher to determine students' mastery of large domains of content.

**11**

Mr. Black, an ENL teacher, was assigned to a new elementary school with a diverse student population. To teach effectively, Mr. Black wanted to learn his students' backgrounds.

Which activity should Mr. Black require his students to help him with his goal?

A) Letting students show on a class map his or her place of birth.

B) Requiring each student to create an identity collage and share it with the class

C) Making a graphic organizer with information about his or her country of origin

D) Bring a traditional family dish.

**12**

Which of the following type of testing regularly assesses students for systematic change or improvement?

A) Achievement test

B) Internal testing

C) Interim assessment

D) Dynamic assessment

**13**

Ms. Lucas, a sixth-grade ENL teacher, is eager to help her beginning-level students to become better in their listening comprehension skills.

Which strategy is best to use to help Ms. Lucas accomplish her desire?

A) Teach students various ways to ask clarifications to the speaker

B) Let students use electronic translators to know unfamiliar phrases

C) Emphasize to students the importance of maintaining eye contact with the speaker

D) Provide written transcripts of daily lessons

**14**

Which of the following gives some ways to improve students' reading, writing, listening and speaking skills?

A) Asking questions and criticizing students work

B) Listening to the students

C) Encouraging discussion

D) All of the above

**15**

To help students evaluate their group's strengths and weaknesses, which cooperative learning technique can be used?

A) Which of the following defines the role of a teacher in a student-centered environment?

B) Law enforcer who makes sure students are following the rules and regulations

C) Co-teacher who works alongside the students to deliver lessons

D) The organizer who monitors and supports student activities

E) The dictator who tells students what to do and controls all their actions

**16**

In Ms. Murray 's English class, the students were asked to predict the outcome of a story. The students were given one minute to think of their predictions before they have been invited to share with a partner their ideas. Some students then voluntarily describe to the whole class their predictions.

Which instructional strategy was used in the situation?

A) The anticipation guide strategy

B) The reciprocal teaching strategy

C) The shared reading strategy

D) The think-pair-share strategy

53          CONTINUE ▶

**17**

Which of the statements below is most agreeable to poor reading ability?

A) It is a problem that students can naturally overcome as they mature.

B) It implies that teachers are not teaching the students.

C) It can bring a lifetime negative impact on the lives of the students.

D) It does not affect children.

**18**

A group of English-speaking toddlers who don't know how to read and write is asked to "do something on the piece of paper."

Which of following the majority of groups will do?

A) Mark the paper

B) Write shape of letters

C) Create scratch that resembles the writing system to which they have been exposed

D) Will do nothing

**19**

Specific warning signs, varying by age and grade, can help teachers flag a student's learning disabilities.

Which of the following is a significant indicator that a first grader might have a problem with reading?

A) Guessing at the spelling of words too much

B) Reading very fast

C) Being bored while reading

D) None of the above

**20**

Which of the following learning opportunities is most likely to promote the development of initiative in kindergarten students?

A) Providing students with charts to self-monitor their progress

B) Assigning responsibility for selected classroom tasks to students

C) Giving students ongoing feedback about their progress

D) Encouraging students to self-select center time activities

At the beginning of the school year, a kindergarten teacher becomes aware that some students in the class have had little or no exposure to text. The teacher aims to encourage students' literacy skills.

Which of the following should be the teacher's first step to use a popular children's book?

A) To illustrate how letters of the alphabet are used to form words.

B) To demonstrate page orientation and other features such as the cover and title.

C) To point out how words are used to form sentences.

D) To show how capital letters and punctuation signal the beginning and end of sentences.

## 22

A starfish live in the sea. Most starfish have five arms. When an arm is lost, the starfish will grow another one.

Which of the following groups of categories did the teacher most likely consider when selecting the text above for a guided reading lesson for her first-grade class?

A) Author's purpose, text structure, and connections

B) Decodable patterns, sight words, and reader interest

C) Word formation, new science concept, and the cause-and-effect relationship

D) Vocabulary level, sentence complexity, and reader's background knowledge

**23**

The fifth-grade teacher wants to form a community of people outside the classroom that will support students' learning.

This can be achieved most adequately by extending the fellowship group in which of the following ways?

A) Teaching other teachers on campus how to implement the fellowship plan.

B) Using college students instead of peers as academic buddies for English Language Learners.

C) Adding fellow buddy and bus fellow responsibilities to the plan

D) Recruiting parents to serve as fellows to the parents of English Language Learners

**24**

Which of the following informal assessment tools would be most useful for documenting a preschool child's ability to perform specific skills?

A) An interview

B) A worksheet

C) A rating scales and shared meaning

D) A running record to identify patterns in student reading

**25**

Which of the following is not considered as a use of standardized assessments?

A) To evaluate whether students have learned what they are expected to learn

B) To determine whether educational policies are working as intended

C) To identify gaps in student learning and academic progress

D) To use standardized test results to alter classroom curriculum

**26**

A fifth-grade teacher has a conference scheduled with one of her student's mother. To ensure a positive, productive meeting, which of the following should the teacher do?

A)  Limiting the meeting to a discussion of specific points that relate to the student's performance in class.

B)  Making a well-supported argument for her views if challenged by the mother.

C)  Assuring her that all instructional decisions regarding her child will be consistent with their values

D)  Listening to what mother says with an open mind and respond in a non-confrontational manner.

**27**

A student is disturbed that another student will not share the computer during the center time.

Which of the following responses by the teacher is most likely to help build a positive classroom community?

A)  Asking the students to work together at a center other than the computer center

B)  Acknowledging the student's feelings and asking both students to suggest possible solutions

C)  Setting a timer and telling both students to switch places on the computer when the timer rings

D)  Reminding both students of the importance of being considerate of others

**28**

Student reports that another student in the class is carrying a pocketknife.

Which of the following actions would be most appropriate for the teacher to take?

A) Contact the school administrator immediately to remove the student from the classroom.

B) Request that the accused student come into the hall and empty all pockets.

C) Advise the student's parents of the report and ask how they wish the situation to be handled.

D) Investigate the incident further by seeking corroboration of the report from other students.

**29**

An elementary school and a community college start a tutoring program. Volunteer college students will be tutoring elementary school students who need extra help.

Which of the following teaching strategies will be the most effective for the tutors in supporting the elementary students' learning?

A) Supplying tutors with a detailed curriculum

B) Providing tutors with ongoing training and support

C) Requesting tutors to write a report after each class

D) Requesting tutors to write detailed lesson plans before each tutoring session

**30**

For promoting the sense of competence and motivation to learn in all students, which of the following strategy is the best use by a second-grade teacher?

A) Differentiating instructions to present each student with tasks that are achievable with persistence

B) Emphasizing homogenous grouping to reduce comparison between students performance at different levels

C) Offering praise for work completion

D) Creating frequent opportunities for friendly competitions

**31**

A teacher from Public Middle School is planning the social studies project in which students will discuss with their community about their childhood and school experiences. Students will present their conclusions to the class with a report.

Which of the following will this project most likely develop?

A) An awareness of the diversity of educational experiences within their community.

B) An understanding of the relationship between community history and current events.

C) An awareness of the variety of resources available in the community.

D) An understanding of how individuals can influence the development of a community.

**32**

A teacher asks students to predict the outcome of a story and tells their partners their predictions after one minute and have some of them described to the class.

Which of the following did the students make use of during this activity?

A) Reciprocal teaching

B) Think-pair-share

C) Shared reading

D) Anticipation guide

**33**

Which of the following is a chronic condition that affects millions of children and often continues into adulthood and includes a combination of persistent problems, such as difficulty sustaining attention, hyperactivity and impulsive behavior?

A) ADD

B) Attention Deficit Disorder

C) ODD

D) All of above

**34**

A student is very upset that another student will not share the computer during the center time.

Which of the following responses by the teacher is most likely to help build a positive classroom community?

A) Asking the students to work together at a center other than the computer center

B) Acknowledging the student's feelings and asking both students to suggest possible solutions

C) Setting a timer and telling both students to switch places at the computer when the timer rings

D) Reminding both students of the importance of being considerate of others

**35**

**Reflective teaching** is a process where teachers think over their teaching practices, changes or improvements for better learning outcomes.

Which of the following is the primary purpose of reflective teaching?

A) To create better curriculum

B) To create a better learning environment

C) To increase parent support for the classroom

D) To critique and improve teaching strategies

**36**

Which of the following is the least important feature of a text and skills that need to be taught to a student in reading comprehension?

A) Memorizing important vocabulary

B) Looking for visuals

C) Notating and analyzing the title

D) Looking up the definition of essential or unknown vocabulary

**37**

By considering which of the following first can the teacher prepare an effective lesson plan for a new instructional unit?

A) Unit activities best for individual and group work

B) The ways unit supports the goals of the district curriculum in this subject area

C) Background knowledge the students already have with regard to the unit topic

D) The most efficient way to evaluate students' achievement of unit objectives

38

You are given the following sentence. Out of the options below, which one indicates best if there is an English grammar problem with it?

When you work up a sweat, you release endorphins, immediately upping your happyness levels.

A) "happyness" should be "happiness"

B) "work up" should be "workout"

C) "your" should be "you're"

D) There are no grammar problems

39

Alice noticed that all of the chairs in her science and literature classrooms are red. She thinks that all of the chairs in all of the classes must also be red.

What kind of reasoning is Alice using in the paragraph given above?

A) Deductive reasoning

B) Logical reasoning

C) Sequential reasoning

D) Inductive reasoning

**40**

While reading a story to first graders about a family going on a weekend camping trip together, the teacher notices that Karen, a child whose parents have recently divorced, has become upset. After speaking with Karen privately and notifying her parents about her reaction, the teacher makes a point the following day of reading a book about a child living with his mother during the week and with his father on the weekends.

What is the importance of reading these two contrasting stories to the students?

I. Every child to see his or her lifestyle reflected and represented in the classroom.

II. The teacher to maintain positive home-school relations and be sure that parents/guardians see their children enjoying school.

III. Children to see that fictional stories sometimes reflect real-life situations.

IV. Karen to know that her peers accept her and see her as having a typical family experience, even if she does not feel positive about it.

A) I and III only
B) II and IV only
C) I and II only
D) III and IV only

# SECTION 4

| # | Answer | Topic | Subtopic | # | Answer | Topic | Subtopic | # | Answer | Topic | Subtopic | # | Answer | Topic | Subtopic |
|---|---|---|---|---|---|---|---|---|---|---|---|---|---|---|---|
| 1 | C | TD | SD2 | 11 | B | TB | SB1 | 21 | B | TB | SB2 | 31 | A | TB | SB3 |
| 2 | D | TB | SB2 | 12 | D | TB | SB1 | 22 | B | TD | SD1 | 32 | D | TB | SB1 |
| 3 | C | TD | SD1 | 13 | A | TB | SB1 | 23 | C | TB | SB3 | 33 | D | TD | SD1 |
| 4 | D | TB | SB1 | 14 | A | TB | SB1 | 24 | C | TB | SB1 | 34 | B | TB | SB1 |
| 5 | D | TD | SD1 | 15 | C | TB | SB2 | 25 | D | TB | SB1 | 35 | D | TB | SB2 |
| 6 | C | TB | SB1 | 16 | D | TB | SB1 | 26 | D | TB | SB3 | 36 | A | TD | SD1 |
| 7 | B | TB | SB1 | 17 | C | TD | SD1 | 27 | B | TB | SB2 | 37 | C | TB | SB1 |
| 8 | D | TD | SD1 | 18 | C | TD | SD1 | 28 | A | TB | SB3 | 38 | A | TD | SD2 |
| 9 | A | TD | SD1 | 19 | A | TD | SD1 | 29 | B | TB | SB1 | 39 | D | TB | SB2 |
| 10 | A | TD | SD1 | 20 | D | TB | SB2 | 30 | B | TB | SB1 | 40 | A | TD | SD1 |

# Topics & Subtopics

| Code | Description | Code | Description |
|---|---|---|---|
| SB1 | Instructional Strategies | SD2 | Language Development |
| SB2 | Professional Development | TB | Professional Environment |
| SB3 | Communication | TD | Language & Literacy Development |
| SD1 | Reading Comprehension | | |

CONTINUE ▶

Made in the USA
Coppell, TX
22 June 2022

79121329R00039